IN THE PRESENCE OF GOD

"In the presence of God" May it happen in your marriage. What a blessing it will be for your partnership in the Gospel. May your faith grow in Jesus as you walk together in The presence of Jesus!

God Bless you always!

Christ Is Risen! He is Risen indeed~ Alleluia

~~~

Presented to

Kristen + James
April 29, 2017

~~~

by

Peeter + Audrey Black

_____

In the Presence of God

Devotions for the Newly Married

Otto W. Toelke

CONCORDIA PUBLISHING HOUSE · SAINT LOUIS

7   8   9   10   11   13

FOREWORD

The story is told of a young lady who was terribly nervous about her upcoming wedding. She asked her mother for advice, especially for the actual wedding day.

"When you walk down that aisle," the mother said, "I want you to think only of three things. First, I want you to think of the word *aisle* and of the many times you walked down the aisle on Sunday morning, excited to hear the Word of God.

"Second, I want you to think of the word *altar* and how it represents the presence of God in the church. Just remember, Jesus is there at your wedding and also goes with you in your marriage.

"Third, I want you to look at the man you're about to marry and think only of *him*.

Think how wonderful your life together will be!"

The young lady religiously followed her mother's instructions. On her wedding day, all the way down the aisle, people could hear her saying to herself, "aisle … altar … him."

There were many smiles on the faces of the wedding guests as she repeated over and over, "aisle … altar … him."

Although the young lady was more than likely not thinking she could alter her husband, many brides and grooms believe they can change their spouses once they're married. We cannot bring about any real change in another person because change comes in only one way—through the transforming power of the Holy Spirit.

There are two purposes for coming into God's presence through these devotions: 1) to recall the promises you made on your wedding day, and 2) to grow in your love for God and for each other as the Holy Spirit works through the Word of God.

If we're honest, most of us were probably too nervous on our wedding day to hear or remember the vows we spoke or the promises we made. Many of us were as nervous as the young woman in the illustration. Some of us may even have come down the aisle thinking we could actually alter our spouse.

Use these devotions to help you review what you said and promised to each other on your wedding day. This review may nudge you to change some things you're doing or saying in your marriage that aren't good or helpful. It may affirm some of the things you're doing or saying that are positive and helpful. Or it might simply help you rejoice and give thanks that God has helped you faithfully keep the promises you made and that He continues to guide and direct you.

We have used these devotions for our personal devotional life and we have been blessed. Each day they seemed to give us a word we needed to hear—a word of comfort, of forgiveness, of joy. We are sure that they will enrich your marriage also.

As you study the Word of God individually or together, the Holy Spirit will be working. Empirical evidence shows that couples who live in the Word of God and who pray have healthier marriages and are less likely to divorce. Jesus reminded the disciples that the words He spoke to them were "spirit and ... life" (John 6:63). When the disciples were asked whether they would leave Jesus, Peter answered, "Lord, to whom shall we go? You have the words of eternal life" (John 6:68). His words give life eternal and life "to the full," including better marriages (John 10:10).

Finally, as you use these devotions, remember that marriage requires work. Lady Chesterfield once said, "My child, if you finally decide to let a man kiss you, put your whole heart into it. No man (or woman!) likes to kiss a rock." A good marriage requires putting your whole heart, mind, and soul into it. One way to do that is to do the very thing you're doing right now—spending time in prayer and meditation, to be, as the very title of this book says, *In the Presence of God!*

May God bless you as you walk together in His presence.

Roger and Robin Sonnenberg

PREFACE

This little volume requires some explanation. While we like to think that it can be profitably read by all, it has as its special target the married couple. The devotions are based on phrases taken from the marriage ceremony. If the devotions are put to use in the early stages of a marriage, then the words of the ceremony are more likely to be remembered and to strike a responsive cord.

These devotions are intended to get husband and wife started in the practice of family devotions. There is an old German maxim which, loosely translated, says, "A good beginning is half the victory." If the couple begin their marriage by regularly and freely speaking to each other about the things of God and of the spirit, this is, indeed, good and augurs well for the future of the marriage.

If acknowledgments for motivation to write these devotions were to be recorded, I would have to place at the top of the list the hundreds of young couples I was privileged to serve as a marital counselor during my years in the parish ministry.

I send forth this little volume with an honest and deep sense of its many shortcomings but with the sincere prayer that it will help bring to some the blessing that the bride and groom at the wedding of Cana enjoyed more than 1,900 years ago. Christ was a guest in their home from its very beginning.

Otto W. Toelke

The Magic of Marriage

The beautiful and impressive words of the marriage ceremony, "We are assembled here in the presence of God and these witnesses to join together this man and this woman in holy matrimony …" still ring in your ears. It has been only a short time since the pastor announced to God and the world that from this day forward you will live as one person. You will not only share with each other, but you will give to each other all that it is possible for you to give of love, of spirit, and of understanding.

It was a beautiful ceremony. It was almost like magic. You entered the church unmarried, and then, within a matter of minutes, everything in your lives suddenly changed. Before there were two hearts, two minds, two spirits. Then, suddenly, as you left the church, it was—and this is not as unreal as it may sound—one heart, one mind, and one spirit. Never, as long as either shall live, can your thoughts about the things that really matter in life exclude the welfare of the other.

The union of husband and wife is close and intimate. Indeed, it is one of the strongest of human bonds. It was designed by the heavenly Architect. You entered this union, as the ceremony says, "in the presence of God." You need never be frightened and the union will never be threatened or broken as long as you remain in the presence of God.

Our Savior Jesus Christ, who gave Himself into death for our sins and rose again victoriously from that death, has given us the blessed assurance that His presence is available to us at all times. In His holy Word He tells us, "And surely, I am with you always, to the very end of the age" (Matthew 28:20).

If the presence of God is lost, it is not because He withdraws from us, but because we, by our sins, withdraw from Him. Your marriage was sealed in the presence of God. He wanted it that way. You wanted it that way. Resolve in these first days of your marriage that, with His help, you will do everything to keep it in the presence of God.

Prayer

Dear Lord, You can do all things. Without You we can do nothing. We ask You to keep us always in Your loving presence. It was our joy to stand hand in hand before Your holy altar and ask You to bless our marriage to Your glory and our good. It is our hope that some day, because of what You have done for us, we will stand hand in hand in the fullness of joy at Your right hand. Amen.

HOW IT ALL BEGAN

Have you ever tried to explain the origin of marriage apart from God? It is difficult to do. Anthropologists and sociologists, studying the origin and development of human beings and society, glibly write that the male and the female were driven together by sheer biological impulse or necessity, or by the herding instinct; that there were certain animal passions or drives in both male and female, and seeing themselves as physically complementing each other, they were naturally drawn together.

One man of God made the statement that when we attempt to explain the origin of marriage in this particular way, we soon find ourselves using the language of the barnyard. Such an explanation, the one apart from God, tends to degrade humanity and marriage.

Is it not much more credible and beautiful

to take the Holy Record as we find it in the very first book of the Bible (Genesis 2:18, 21–24): "The LORD God said, 'It is not good for the man to be alone. I will make a helper suitable for him.' … So the LORD God caused the man to fall into a deep sleep; and while he was sleeping, He took one of the man's ribs and closed up the place with flesh. Then the LORD God made a woman from the rib He had taken out of the man, and He brought her to the man. The man said, 'This is now bone of my bones and flesh of my flesh; she shall be called "woman" for she was taken out of man.' For this reason a man will leave his father and mother and be united to his wife, and they will become one flesh."

This simple but mysterious, this beautiful and profound record of the origin of marriage is the one Christians accept. We not only accept it, but cling to it. First, the Bible record makes us think of ourselves and our spouses as children of God rather than brutes or animals. Second, the Bible record puts into marriage not only the purpose of propagation, but the high and noble purposes of the divine order.

Some may say that they do not leave God out of the picture, but that they cannot believe that He operated so directly in the lives of humans. They have forgotten that He did so when He Himself became man, came down to earth in the form of the Savior Christ, and suffered and died for the sins of the world. And some day He will claim as His own all who believe.

Prayer

Dear Father in heaven, we believe that we are the creatures of Your word and the work of Your hands. You created us. You created the marriage relationship. You placed us in it. Help us to keep this relationship as high and as holy as You intended it to be. We ask in Jesus' name. Amen.

WHAT DO YOU MEAN— *HOLY* MATRIMONY?

Have you ever taken the time to page through the dictionary and look up the word *matrimony*? A good dictionary will tell you that in addition to the married state, or wedlock, the word matrimony can refer also to a game of cards and to the combination of a king and a queen in some games.

Humorists, with their satire and irony, could, of course, give us any number of definitions that are amusing but hardly enlightening or inspiring.

In the marriage ceremony the words "to join together this man and this woman in holy matrimony" were spoken. It is not absolutely necessary that you have a profound understanding of the word *matrimony* in order for your marriage to be successful and God-pleasing, but it is important that you are aware of, and have a reasonable understanding of, the word that immediately precedes the word *matrimony* in the Christian marriage ceremony. That is, of course, the word *holy*.

An offhand and rule-of-thumb definition for the word *holy* is "without sin." Since you were united in *holy* matrimony, does this mean that your marriage is without sin? The answer is yes and no. No—your marriage is not holy, for neither your marriage nor any other marriage ever consummated on the face of the earth has been without sin. Since the components themselves, the man and the woman who go into marriage, are sinful, the whole that comes from the union must also be sinful. Yes—your marriage is holy because it was instituted by the most high God, because the estate was blessed by Him, because it was performed in His presence, but most of all, it is holy because Jesus, the Son of God Himself, imputes, attributes, or ascribes to the husband and wife who believe in Him the holiness or righteousness that He so dearly earned on Calvary's cross.

The Bible clearly states, "All our righteous acts are like filthy rags" (Isaiah 64:6). More simply put, it means that without Christ there is no good in us. So also, without Christ your marriage can only be unholy matrimony. It becomes *holy* matrimony only when each marriage partner kneels in humble obedience before the Savior of all, confesses sins against both God and others, and receives forgiveness. This means that the sins have been removed, that a state of holiness in Christ exists. Only in this sense can two people live in the estate of *holy* matrimony.

Prayer

Dear heavenly Father, we know that You have set a standard for our lives. "Be holy because I, the LORD your God, am holy" (Leviticus 19:2). Grant that in our marriage we will never seek this holiness in ourselves or in each other, where it can never be found. You have promised though that if we, on bended knees, with bowed heads, and with humble hearts, seek our holiness in Christ, Your Son and our Savior, we will never be disappointed. Cause us always to search in the right place for that holiness that we so much want and so seldom use. Amen.

YOU GET MORE THAN A SPOUSE

When you, as Christians, chose each other as lifelong companions and partners in marriage, it was assumed that the choice was not made unadvisedly or lightly. Sometimes it is. There are those who regard marriage as a mere social arrangement. If the arrangement is not pleasing and satisfying, then, they feel, society furnishes them with an escape called divorce, and presto! the problem is solved.

However, even among those whose attitude is Christian and wholesome, there are times when holy matrimony is entered into unadvisedly or lightly. This comes about not by indifference, but rather by a lack of understanding of the many facets of human personality.

A nationally known marriage counselor put it this way: "Do you know that when you pick your life companion you are choosing a habit system, a cultural background, a set of loyalties, and a life philosophy? These should be understood and accepted."

Habits, culture, loyalties, and philosophy are things that are not easily or quickly changed or altered. Usually these are either good or bad attributes of an individual that have been molded in the crucible of heredity and environment over the years.

If your marriage partner's conduct or thinking at times seems irregular or unusual or even distasteful to you, perhaps it is so only in the light of your background. Also, you should remember that this works both ways.

Just because a culture—and "culture" is a broad and all-inclusive term that includes everything from diet and dress to music and customs—is different from the one in which you were raised, that does not mean it is inferior or no good.

Every individual is a product of the world he or she has known, the people with whom he or she associated, the economic conditions under which he or she existed, the recreation he or she enjoyed, and the religious influence under which he or she lived.

To the degree that you overlook or disregard these factors in your relationship with your spouse, you could be entering the state of holy matrimony unadvisedly or lightly. Bear in mind the fabric of your marriage was fashioned from a thousand sources.

Prayer

Dear Lord Jesus, we know that the Gospel of salvation that You secured for us by Your death and resurrection transcends all things. It cannot be limited by custom, race, or culture. Make our love for each other like that. Make it so noble, warm, and true that when people see it in action they will think of Your greater love. Amen.

The Two Will Become One
Matthew 19:5

Two in One

"Marriage is a fifty-fifty proposition." How many times have you heard people make that statement? Some make the statement in all seriousness, honestly believing that if the proposition is always borne in mind, then marriage is invulnerable; no matter how many pitfalls, it will survive them all.

If marriage is nothing more than a "fifty-fifty" relationship, then we may as well reduce the whole thing to a business contract. But God never intended marriage merely as a contract. Nowhere in Scripture do we find a passage indicating that in marriage all property is to be jointly owned by husband and wife, or that all responsibility is to be equally shared, or that each spouse is to have the same amount of leisure time and recreation, or that there is to be a distinct division of labor, or no division of labor. Perhaps the reason the Bible never mentions these things is simply because the Creator thought of and described marriage in far more noble, intimate, and personal terms. He said, "... and the two will become one." In the sight of God, and therefore in the sight of the Christian, marriage is far more a union than it is a contract. It is the blending and bonding together of two people, spiritually, emotionally, socially, and physically. A contract is an instrument that forces one to carry out the conditions of an agreement. Marriage is an instrument of God used to bring two people into the closest harmony that human beings can know.

If you ever permit yourselves to take marriage from the high plane on which God Himself placed it, then you are downgrading a divine union to an earthly association.

What it means to become *one* with someone else is very difficult to express in words. Jesus, our Savior, became *one* with man when He left His heavenly throne in the incarnation. In so doing He felt the hurt of humiliation, the pain of poverty, the degradation of deceit, the leaden load of loneliness, the sickness of sin, and the doom of death. He never complained that He was being pushed beyond the requirements of a *contract.* He also felt, and made it possible for us to feel, the throbbing heart of a loving God.

God, in Christ, became *one* with man so that some day man might be at home in the presence of God.

When a Christian husband and wife "become one," they assuredly cannot do for each other what Christ has done for every sinner, but they can constantly point to what has been done by Christ. This cannot be brought about by contractual agreement. Only a union permeated with Christian love can make two people *one* in the way in which Christ speaks of it.

Prayer

O Jesus, in Your incarnation You chose to become one with us. We cannot truly understand why You make this choice, but we are deeply grateful for it. When You became one with us, our sins became Your sins and Your victory became ours. Grant that our marriage relationship may pattern itself in oneness after You. Amen.

❦

What … God Has Joined Together
Matthew 19:6

"HOW DO I LOVE THEE?"

How do I love thee? Let me count the ways.
    I love thee to the depth and breadth and
        height
    My soul can reach, when feeling out of sight
For the ends of Being and ideal Grace.
I love thee to the level of every day's
    Most quiet need, by sun and candlelight.
    I love thee freely, as men strive for Right;
I love thee purely, as they turn from Praise.
I love thee with the passion put to use
    In my old griefs, and with my childhood's
        faith.
I love thee with a love I seemed to lose
    With my lost saints,—I love thee with the
        breath,
Smiles, tears, of all my life!—and, if God choose,
    I shall but love thee better after death.

You do not have to be a well-read and cultured individual to see the quiet beauty and feel the warm depth of Elizabeth Browning's words. She wrote the sonnet to her husband.

From this sonnet and other literary works from this particular period in English literature, we may assume that people in that day believed in the theory of "personal affinity"—the theory that two people were intended only for each other. If one of them married a person with whom he or she did not have this "personal affinity," the results could be only disappointing and tragic.

If we take seriously the lyrics of many popular love songs, we would have to assume that there are still many people who believe in the theory of "personal affinity." They may not say it in their own words, but they borrow the words of a song or express the thought that each man must have one specific woman and that each woman must have one certain man. If, among all the people in the world, these two people do not find each other but settle for someone else, a tragic mismatch takes place.

The whole idea makes wonderful material for songwriters and poets, but if we examine the situation we would have to admit that the theory is more romantic than factual.

Yet if we recall the words from the marriage ceremony, "what God has joined together," we Christians cannot but feel that we, as husband and wife, have been brought together by greater and more discerning forces than mere chance and accident. For the Christian the feeling is real and valid.

Because you are Christians, there were prayers uttered, vows exchanged, and blessings bestowed before your actual marriage. God was in the picture ever and always.

Even if you do not believe that you have a "personal affinity" for each other, you have expressed the belief that you each have a "personal affinity" in and for Christ. In Him, the Head, you are joined as members of the same body. This is a union that by far transcends any union expressed in poem or song. Your marriage is a union designed by God, blessed by Christ, and sustained by the working of the Holy Spirit in your lives. Yes, as Christian husband and wife you are meant specifically for each other because you are two who "God has joined together."

Prayer

Dear Lord, although we in no way deserve it, You have showered countless blessings upon us. You have given us each other as husband and wife. May our marriage, as we live it, always show that it was begun, designed, and directed by You. When our relationship as husband and wife becomes strained because of our weaknesses and sins, cause us to remember that the real cement that binds our marriage is our oneness in the body of Christ. Make us obedient and responsive members of that body. Amen.

WHAT ABOUT MY PARENTS?

Upon entering the marriage relationship and establishing your own home, another relationship comes to an end. The relationship of the bride and groom to their parents is deeply changed. True, a son never ceases to be a son, and a daughter never ceases to be a daughter, but the relationship has changed.

The parental home, which once was the center of love and affection, which once offered more security than anyplace in the world, which once was a place of multiplying joys and sharing sorrows, has now been supplanted by the newly established home of bride and groom. A young husband cannot think of his parents in exactly the same way he did before. The focal point of his love has changed and now concentrates upon his wife. A young wife cannot feel toward her parents exactly as she did before. Her husband has now become her first love. This is as it should be.

However, Christian newlyweds never cease to honor their fathers and their mothers. They never permit their new love for each other, which by its very nature is different in kind, to make them oblivious to the parental love and concern that, in most cases, has sustained them to the day of their marriage.

This change in relationships, this shifting of affections, is an adjustment that entails real perils for many couples. Count the marriages that know unnecessary discord because the young bride is "tied to her mother's apron strings." Count the marriages that lose their sparkle because he is "a mama's boy." Their number is legion, and they are found in all classes of society.

A Christian should make the adjustment with a minimum of emotional disturbance. He knows that God wants him always to love, honor, and respect his parents. She knows that, humanly speaking, she will never be able to repay her parents for all that they have done for her. But she ought never permit her filial love or sense of obligation to detract from that love which she has pledged to her spouse.

As an illustration in this matter let us consider Christ in His relationship to the church. He never married, and yet He had a bride—the church. When Mary, His mother, interfered, although unknowingly, with His services of love to His bride (on the occasion of the twelve-year-old Jesus in the temple and again at the wedding at Cana), Jesus lovingly but firmly informed her that His first task was to show the way of salvation to a world gripped in sin. He never ceased to love Mary. Even on the cross He was concerned about her welfare. But first in His life was His bride, the church, those who believe in Him for the forgiveness of their sins.

Prayer

Dear Savior, we have in our lives developed and nourished wholesome loyalties to parents, relatives, and special friends. Teach us to maintain these without interfering with the even greater loyalty that we have to each other as husband and wife. Teach us that loyalties do not have to be in conflict, but that they can add a new dimension to our lives. Above all, cause us always to be loyal to You, our Lord and our God. Amen.

And They Shall Be One Flesh

WHO PUT THE HEX ON SEX?

A pastor was once preaching to a group of young people about the place of sex in the life of the Christian. The title of his sermon was "Who Put the Hex on Sex?" A catchy little phrase, indeed! If we stop to think about it, it soon becomes apparent that these few words get right to the core of the problem quicker than some books that have been written on problems of sex.

Sex is an extremely important and determining factor in the life of every individual. It is not Christian to attempt to hide or ignore the matter of sex. In marriage it is such an ever-present and important factor that the success or failure of the marriage may be determined by the attitude of husband and wife toward it.

Prior to your marriage, by divine wisdom

clearly expressed in Scripture, you were told to exercise cautious restraint in matters of sex. In the moment when you were pronounced husband and wife what was before forbidden became permissible within the bounds of propriety. Certain rights and privileges in the area of sex that are sharply forbidden outside marriage become permissible within marriage. This adjustment to the marriage relationship is not easy for everyone.

This is not God's fault. This is not the fault of sex. It is because of the hex. How did the hex come about? As always, it is simply another case of human beings taking the beautiful things of God and twisting and distorting them into something evil. For example, morphine can be a welcome blessing to someone in pain, or it can be a torturing curse to an individual addicted to drugs.

There is nothing wrong in sex itself. God Himself created it and placed it in Adam and Eve. The Bible record is very clear, simple, and beautiful (Genesis 2:24–25): "… and they will become one flesh. The man and his wife were both naked, and they felt no shame."

This does not mean that God placed no

restrictions on sex. In fact, God placed restrictions on everything in life, especially the beautiful things. If they became commonplace, they would no longer be beautiful.

May God grant that in your marriage the physical or sexual relationship will always be a thing of beauty, within the restrictions of God's holy Word. If and when either partner of the marriage momentarily loses this God-given perspective of sex, let him or her remember that the Savior died for all sins—including the sins against the Sixth Commandment—and ask for forgiveness.

Prayer

Dear Father in heaven, in our sinful times it is so easy to become confused in matters pertaining to sex. We so often find ourselves vacillating between prudery and permissiveness, between joy and guilt. We forget that sex is a natural gift that You embodied in both man and woman to better enable them to express their love for each other. Grant that even in the intimate relationship of sex we live to the glory of Your holy name. Amen.

PLANNED PARENTHOOD

A Protestant church body gathered in convention drew up a series of 13 summary statements on "Marriage and Family Life." These statements were to be used as guidelines. Statement number four reads in part: "Husband and wife are called to exercise the power of procreation responsibly before God. This implies planning their parenthood in accordance with their ability to provide for their children and carefully nurture them in fullness of Christian faith and life. The health and welfare of the mother-wife should be a major concern in such decisions. Irresponsible conception of children up to the limit of biological capacity and selfish limitation of the number of children are equally detrimental."

If a heading had been furnished for the 13 statements, it would have been "Birth

Control," or "Planned Parenthood," as many prefer to call it.

When it comes to applying this statement to your married life, there are yet many questions to be answered. When is the conception of children "irresponsible"? This is a relative thing, and therefore only you two people, as Christian husband and wife, can give the answer that applies in your case. When does the limitation of the number of children become "selfish"? Again, this is a relative thing and only you, as Christian husband and wife, can furnish the answer.

God has given His children a great deal of freedom in certain areas. This is one of them. But freedom does not mean license to do as we please. It means the right to make a choice in accordance with God's will for us. Under freedom we sometimes choose what our sinful nature desires.

If the size of your family is to be determined only by unbridled sexual indulgence, or on the other hand only by the selfish thought of how much it will cost in time and money if you do have children, then you will not have learned how to properly use the freedom God has given you.

As in all things, discuss this matter freely with each other and in your prayers to God. In a multitude of ways He will give you His divine direction.

Prayer

O Father in heaven, whose family fills both heaven and earth, give us, we pray, divine wisdom and direction as we plan our family. Conception and birth, life and death, are in Your hands. We are tools to be used to fulfill Your purposes. Make us, in our thoughts, words, and deeds, worthy of this privilege and service. Amen.

⋘∾⋙

Your Wife Will Be like a Fruitful Vine, Your Children like Olive Plants around Your Table

CONTINUING HIS CREATION

This was the psalmist's way of telling what the attitude of the Christian husband and wife is to be toward children. (See Psalm 128.) The beautiful picture that he draws is quite a contrast to many present-day attitudes. We have heard parents refer to their children not as olive plants but as tax exemptions or the unpleasant, inevitable consequences of the marriage relationship.

The Christian husband and wife can take only a very positive attitude toward children. The Christian couple feels this way not only because reproduction and the care of children is one of the reasons God instituted the holy estate of matrimony, they feel this way because they regard children as a gift of God. (There was a time when some sections of the Christian church taught that reproduction is the primary, if not the sole, purpose of marriage. This cannot be true because sometimes, contrary to all desires and efforts, marriages remain childless, but they remain marriages nevertheless.)

When God permits you to have children, He is honoring you by letting you carry out His continuing creation. Children are, in a very real sense, the crown that God places on the estate of holy matrimony. Down through the ages Christians have always recognized children as a gift of God. They have indicated this in many ways—by the names they bestowed (e.g., Theodore means "gift of God"), by the care they give their children, and by their efforts, already when the child was a tender age, to instill in him or her the blessed truths of the Gospel.

The whole idea of children being a gift of God fits naturally into the scheme of Christian concepts. The greatest gift that God gave was a Child—His own dear Son. That Son in turn gave His life on Calvary. Why? So that, as you will recall from the marriage ceremony, "May the LORD bless you from Zion all the days of your life; may you see the prosperity of Jerusalem, and may you live to see your children's children. Peace be upon Israel" (Psalm 128:5).

Prayer

Dear Father in heaven, our Creator and Preserver, You alone are "the Giver of every good and perfect gift." In Your good time, and according to Your will, crown our marriage with children, the richest of blessings. Your Son, our Savior, loved little children. He took them up in His arms and blessed them. May His example fashion our attitude. It is in His name that we pray. Amen.

WHY SOME MARRIAGES FAIL

The lyrics of a once-popular song tell us that "love and marriage go together like a horse and carriage," that "you can't have one without the other." If only this were true. If it were, we would not have an appalling percentage of marriages ending in the divorce courts.

Too often we come upon marriages—some of them of long standing—that appear to have been drained and emptied of the very last drop of love and affection. The marriage still exists, but the love has long since disappeared. We, of course, wonder what brought this about.

There are countless reasons why marriages fail. Perhaps one of the most frequent is that, unlike the songwriter who mistakenly made love and marriage synonymous, there are too many couples who differentiate between love and sex.

Are love and sex two different things? Considered from one point of view they are one and the same. From another point of view they are quite different.

In the absolute sense they are different. The best proof of this is that all normal adults feel the strong biological urge that we call sex, but not all experience love in the high sense in which we are using the word. Sex is a biological function—a strong instinctual drive—while love is an emotional experience. Love is not a part of a human's built-in equipment, but sex is. Sex can be, and often is, casual about its object; love cannot be casual about its object. One is a physical experience, the other an emotion.

In another sense love and sex are one and the same thing. This must be the concept and attitude of truly Christian marriage partners. They must have this attitude not only as a safeguard against unfaithfulness, but more so as a guide and mandate in their physical relations with, and approach to, each other. The Christian spouse thinks of sex as a God-given means of expressing love for the marriage partner in a language that transcends words. At the same time the Christian thinks of love as a pleasant restraint that will never permit abuse and degradation of the sexual relationship.

The life of the Christian—and in a special way this applies to the relationship between a Christian husband and wife—can be pictured in the form of a wheel. In the center of this wheel, serving as the very hub, is Christ, whom to know is to love and in whom the love of God Himself is revealed. The spokes emanating from this hub of Christ(ian) love are our intellectual, social, economic, physical, and spiritual relationships. They center in and are governed by Christian love. Sex can no more be torn out of the hub of Christian love without destroying the wheel than can any other phase of human relationships.

Prayer

Dear Father in heaven, in Your Son, Jesus Christ, You have given us an example of perfect love. We know that because we are not perfect, our love for each other as husband and wife cannot be perfect. However, with Your help and guidance we want to express our love for each other in full measure, using mind, and body, and spirit. Help us do this, dear Lord. Amen.

◯◯◯

Who Gives This Woman to Be
Married to This Man?

THE CHAIN OF LIFE

There is a portion of the marriage ceremony that receives little attention, and often references to it are in a joking manner. Have you ever asked why the question "Who gives this woman to be married to this man?" is incorporated in the ceremony? What is the real meaning and purpose of the question?

Actually it is a symbolic way of expressing a deep and profound truth. When a man and woman marry they become part of an endless chain of life. As products of their parents' marriage, they are linked to the past. As potential parents of future offspring, they are linked to the future.

After the father answers the question, he seats himself in the congregation. What a beautifully symbolic way of saying that one generation is receding from the stage of life, a generation that has reared its children and kept the torch of life burning, to make way for a new and younger generation whose progeny will in turn bring new hope and life to a disturbed world. After the father is seated, the new family occupies the center of the stage. They become the leading characters in the great drama of life.

God has given to each generation the responsibility of new life. When the father gives the bride away, we actually witness the passing of the responsibility from one generation to the next.

The endless chain of life of which you have now become a part should not be broken or needlessly weakened by irresponsibility, indifference, or selfishness.

The Savior Himself is our best example of one who preserved the chain of life. By His death He tied together for us the poles of eternity. By His death and resurrection He mended the broken chain between almighty God and sinful humanity. He carried for us the torch of eternal life.

Your generation is now on stage. Look to the Savior for guidance and direction so that you will, in a way purposeful to God and humans, meet your responsibilities.

Prayer

Dear Savior, from the foundations of the world You have called us to membership in Your family. By Your death and resurrection the chain of life that will bring us into the Abiding City has been made strong and sure. Grant that in our generation we will be always aware of our bond to the past and our responsibility to the future. Amen.

Even as Christ Is the Head
of the Church

How Did Jesus Feel About Marriage?

Do you recall that portion of the marriage ceremony taken from Ephesians 5:22–23 which reads, "Wives, submit to your husbands as to the Lord. For the husband is the head of the wife as Christ is the head of the church, His body, of which He is the Savior"? It is a beautiful passage of Scripture because in it the apostle describes the relationship between Christ and His church, and then he places alongside this picture the relationship between spouses and says that there should be a definite similarity.

There was a time in the history of Christianity—that period when church and theologians spoke of marriage as a yielding to temptation and weakness, and at the same time extolled celibacy—when the significance of this comparison was lost. The more we study the pages of Scripture to learn what it has to say about marriage, the more evident it becomes that marriage is not only a divine natural order and a remedy against sin but a state in which the Christian can show how through faith the natural relationships of life can become symbols of Christ's love, trust, and fidelity.

If the Savior had regarded the married state as a sort of "second choice," He most certainly would not have used it to describe His relationship to those for whom He died. He would never have referred to Himself as the Groom, and to His church as the bride.

The Christian bride and groom, by virtue of the comparison that God's Word makes, find themselves brought together in a deep and wonderfully mysterious relationship. It is more than a relationship created by a civil contract or a social adjustment justified by human purposes. It is a relationship that finds its very roots and foundation in the purposes of God and the love of God.

Prayer

Dear Father in heaven, You instituted marriage, Your Son blessed it, and Your Holy Spirit sanctifies it. As a symbol of Christ's relationship to the church, our marriage has a quality and a dignity that is truly beyond our comprehension. Make us and our love for each other worthy of that which our marriage symbolizes. In Jesus' name. Amen.

The Roles of Husbands and Wives
in God's Order—I

THE HUSBAND'S ROLE
IN MARRIAGE

It was only about a century ago—the era of our great-grandparents—when the problems associated with marriage, the family, and the home were given very little attention. They did not require the extensive study and investigation they are receiving today. Society was not nearly as complex as it is today. The economic role, the social status, the physical responsibility, and the division of labor for husband and wife were all quite clearly defined when compared to the mixed and clouded thinking that we have on these matters today.

In the face of all this confusion we find many husbands and wives quite bewildered about their respective responsibilities and duties in the new family unit they are establishing.

Society may change, but God's Word and human nature do not change. The problem is applying God's Word to a changing society.

The husband is the head of the wife. This is the natural order that God Himself ordained. The status of women in Western society has been constantly upgraded since the rise of Christianity. This is an inherent feature of Christianity. But it does not change the natural order that God Himself prescribed.

This has nothing to do with "women's rights," or "the equality of women," or "women's suffrage." These all Christians, male and female, favor as long as they are within the framework of the divine order.

The husband is the head of the wife, not in the sense that his is "the master's voice" in all matters, but in the sense that God has selected him to play a very definite role in the family. He is to give the family strength, stability, security. He is to be the shelter for the other members of the family when the storms of life break.

The husband is the head of the wife, but he exercises this headship only in love. (Billy Sunday once said, "If you want your wife to be an angel, don't treat her like the devil.") The

Christian husband would no more abuse this headship than he would abuse his own body. The understanding Christian wife knows this and finds comfort and wisdom in the divine order.

Prayer

O Lord, cause me as a husband to love my wife even as Christ loved the church. Help me to love my wife as my own body, even as Christ loves us all as members of His body. Amen.

~∞~

The Roles of Husbands and Wives
in God's Order—II

THE WIFE'S ROLE
IN MARRIAGE

In the marriage ceremony there is a question directed to the bride that reads as follows: "Will you love, honor, cherish, *and obey him,* and keep with him this bond of wedlock holy and unbroken till death you do part?" Some pastors have been requested by brides, on occasion, to omit the word "obey." Apparently these brides felt that the word is too strong and ascribes to the husband, by implication, greater authority than they wished to recognize.

Let's be charitable and say that they made the request because they really had not familiarized themselves with the entire ceremony, but permitted themselves the dangerous liberty of tearing a word out of its context and applying their own definition.

What does the Bible say about the position of the wife in the family? The answer is clear and concise—"Now as the church submits to Christ, so also wives should submit to their husbands in everything" (Ephesians 5:24).

Before we begin trying to determine what it means for a wife to submit to her husband, let us not make the mistake, as is so often done, of overlooking the first phrase in the sentence, namely, "as the church submits to Christ."

Was there ever a time when the true church felt that it did not want to submit to Christ? Was there ever a time when Christ, the Head of the church, ruled and governed His flock like a ruthless tyrant? Has there ever been a time when you, as a Christian, have felt that Christ has dealt with you in a loveless, unjust matter? Has there ever been a time when in obeying Christ you were made to feel like a dog obeying its master? Of course, the answer is no. The whole relationship is one of limitless love and not of tyranny and domination.

When the wife submits to her husband, she is fulfilling a very definite role that God has given her. In the home where the husband represents strength, stability, and security, the wife should supply tenderness, compassion, encouragement, beauty, and understanding. The contributions of both are vitally essential to the establishment of a real home.

In a truly Christian family the subject of "who is the head of the family?" never comes up. What should come up in the heart and mind of each of you regularly is this question—"Am I fulfilling the wonderful and unique role that God according to His divine order has given me as a husband or wife?" If both of you can answer this question in the affirmative, you will have no trouble with the husband abusing his headship or with the wife complaining about her submission.

Prayer

O Lord, as in all things, so also in the marriage relationship, You have instituted order. Both husband and wife have different but equally important roles to fill. Even as the true church, Your bride, knows only joy and pleasure in filling the role You have given her, so may I also joyfully fill my role as a wife. Amen.

Your Mutual Consent Sincerely and Freely Given

WHAT'S PAST IS PAST

When you spoke your marriage vows to God and to each other before witnesses, you were giving yourselves to each other as of that day and for all the days to come. Prior to that time, or to your engagement, you had no claim upon each other and you imposed no standards upon each other. Perhaps you know little or nothing about the romance (if there was any) that was in the life of your spouse before you were acquainted. If it has not concerned you until this time, why start inquiring now? If it has concerned you, it's best to forget about it.

Frequently in newspaper columns generally known as "advice to the lovelorn" we read about a young husband or wife who is so persistent in digging into the antemarital past that the marriage partner, in a moment of intimacy, and having the promise that "nothing will matter," tells all. The results are painful and unpleasant. How can they be otherwise? A husband or wife is not required either by God or man to reveal to the spouse all experiences, both good and bad, of premarital days. However, if past sins are revealed, there is the Christian duty of forgiveness. This will be easier if we remember that we are *all* sinners in desperate need of forgiveness.

While it is true that it is not advisable for husband and wife to withhold any great secrets from each other, it is also true that you accepted each other for what you were on the day of your marriage. Even if husband and wife do share with each other their personal, intimate experiences before marriage, they must, as Christians, always guard against sitting in judgment on an incident that took place a long time ago under circumstances that could never be accurately and actually reconstructed.

If the Savior would deal with us this way, our lives would be filled with regret and despair and we never would reach heaven. Through the apostle Paul He tells us what our attitude should be—"Forgetting what is behind and straining toward what is ahead, I press on toward the goal to win the prize for which God has called me heavenward in Christ Jesus" (Philippians 3:13–14).

Prayer

Grant, O Lord, that the happiness that we now know in our marriage may never be marred or disturbed by the past. By the forgiveness that You have granted to each of us we stand before You dressed in the garment of Your righteousness alone. Amen.

WHAT WILL IT BE—TRUST OR SUSPICION?

Perhaps one of the most essential ingredients of a happy and satisfying Christian marriage is the element of trust. Husband and wife, if they are ever to find genuine and abiding peace in their marriage, must have implicit trust in each other. You, as a wife, must be convinced that your husband would never take the love and affection that he has promised to you and give it to another woman. The same applies, of course, to you, the husband, in your relationship with your wife. Never should you permit yourself even to suspect that your spouse might be unfaithful.

When Joseph became aware of the fact that the virgin Mary was to give birth to a child, we do not read that he immediately cast her aside and accused her of adultery. He could well have done this and been faulted by no one. The Bible says, "Then Joseph her husband, being a just man …" (Matthew 1:19 KJV). Soon a messenger direct from God, in the form of an angel, explained the whole situation to trusting Joseph. What would have been interpreted an offensive and unclean relationship on the part of Mary was soon seen for what it really was—the most beautiful plan that God Himself has devised for humanity.

He is not telling us that when a couple is married they need no longer give attention to personal appearance—that they should cease trying to be charming—that they should leave off striving for the social virtues. He does tell us, however, that in the Christian life—and it applies especially to the Christian married life—there is no place for artificiality and pride.

The Christian spouse loves his mate not only because of her fine attributes and virtues, but also because of her faults and weaknesses. The Christian bride does not hesitate to mention a weakness or a shortcoming to her spouse, and such gentle reminders should be taken in the right spirit.

Christian marriage partners should be

humble, honest, and open toward each other. This is one of the great blessings of marriage.

This is one of the reasons true believers, members of the body of Christ, are relaxed, comfortable, and happy in the presence of Christ, the Bridegroom. There is no attempt at deception. Sins are brought out in the open and confessed. Forgiveness is received, and He who hates the sin ever, always shows His love for the sinner.

Clothe yourselves with humility toward each other. It will make your marriage much more comfortable.

Prayer

Dear Lord, whose humility extended even to death and the grave in order that we might have life and have it more abundantly, remove from us all artificiality and pride in our relationship as husband and wife. May our greatest pride be Your presence as a guest in our home. Amen.

I Will Greatly Multiply
Thy Sorrow

HOW TO HANDLE SIN

God Himself made the statement, "I will greatly multiply thy sorrow" (Genesis 3:16 KJV). He directed it to Eve. The statement was probably used in your marriage ceremony when the officiant said, "Hear also the cross which by reason of sin God has laid upon this estate."

The estate of holy matrimony is not immune to sin. It would be well for you at this early period in your married life to discuss what your course will be when sins are committed, and what your strength will be when the consequences of the sins arrive.

We know how to handle sins in our lives, thanks to our gracious and loving Savior, Jesus Christ. It is the same for all people, married or single. First, we confess them to our God. (We may also confess to each other. Husband and wife may well serve each other in the capacity of confessor and confessee.) Second, we ask for forgiveness. Third, we determine to do our utmost, with the help of God, not to fall into the same sin again.

Now, if we believe this, the sin so handled is gone forever—washed away by the blood of the Lamb. The consequence, however, may remain and have to be endured. For example, the sin of reckless driving that led to an accident may be forgiven, but the physical injury that resulted may endure for a lifetime. Where do we find the strength, understanding, and patience to bear such crosses if they occur in our lives? We, of course, lift up our eyes "unto the hills, from whence cometh [our] help" (Psalm 121:1 KJV). The Lord never gives us a burden greater than we can bear. If the burden is heavy, He gives us added strength. Abraham knew this. Moses knew it. David knew it. Peter knew it. Paul knew it. Yes, all the hosts of saints that have gone before knew it. They went to the hill of God's strength for their help. Follow in the footsteps of the saints.

You can share this divine strength with each other and so build each other up in the faith. As fellow believers redeemed by Christ, you constantly hold up each other's hands by sharing the help that you receive at God's holy hill. Just as you like to hear your spouse tell you often that he or she loves you, so also your spouse as a Christian never tires of hearing of the love of God. Reassure each other of God's love.

Prayer

Chief of sinners though I be,
Jesus shed His blood for me,
Died that I might live on high,
Lives that I might never die.
As the branch is to the vine,
I am His, and He is mine. Amen.

Lutheran Worship, 285

For Better, for Worse

WHEN YOU FIND A FAULT
IN YOUR SPOUSE

A man in his seventies went to the doctor for a physical examination. At the conclusion of the examination the doctor pronounced him physically well and healthy and inquired about the rules of health he followed in order to maintain his physical fitness.

The aged gentleman replied, "When my wife and I were married more than fifty years ago, we agreed that whenever she lost her temper because of any fault in me she would keep quiet, and that whenever I would lose my temper because of any fault in her I would take a walk. Perhaps my good health can be attributed to the fact that for more than fifty years I have lived pretty much of an outdoor life."

Yes, it makes us chuckle, but underneath lies the sad reality that here were two people who never accepted their spouse for what he or she really was. For more than half a century they unsuccessfully tried to reform and refashion each other's personalities. The project of "making a new man" or "making a new woman" of your spouse seldom meets with success. Even if it does succeed, it is often questionable if the refashioned personality is an improvement on the original.

There is a wise old saying that reads, "The time to keep both eyes open is before marriage, and the time to keep one eye closed is after marriage." Each must learn to accept the other for what he or she is. In a sense the following well-known prayer is most appropriate when evaluating your spouse: "God grant me the serenity to accept the things I cannot change, the courage to change the things I can, and the wisdom to know the difference."

Even as the sinful person is refashioned and remade to the point where he "grows in grace," not by the stinging whip and cutting sword of God's law, but rather by the love of God as he comes to know it in Jesus Christ, so also the inadequate spouse is not refashioned by carping criticism but rather by loving patience and tender understanding.

Prayer

Dear Savior, even as I have Your divine and eternal love in spite of my many sins and weaknesses, so may my love for my spouse be unaffected by sins and weaknesses. If I too often see the speck in my spouse's eye, remind me of the plank in my own eye. Even as there is always forgiveness with You, so may we always find forgiveness in each other. Amen.

꩜

In Honesty and Industry
to Provide for Each Other

WHO MANAGES THE
MONEY IN THE FAMILY?

As Christian husband and wife you did not enter the estate of holy matrimony for reasons of financial gain. The glib saying, "It's just as easy to love them if they are rich," may be true, but the "rich" part should be only incidental and never the motivating force behind a marriage.

Nevertheless, money and the way in which it is handled is an important factor in every marriage. If either of the marriage partners is irresponsible in this area, the billows of the sea of matrimony can become dangerously tempestuous. An old adage says, "When the wolf is at the door, love flies out the window." Fortunately the adage is only an adage and not at all descriptive of what happens in a truly Christian marriage when the wolf is at the door. Financial problems, as all problems, can strengthen a marriage by bringing husband and wife together in a common cause. Here is a problem that can be solved only by cooperation, understanding, and perseverance.

Difficulties often arise in the family finances when there is too great a disparity in the financial backgrounds of the marriage partners. Two people, even husband and wife, with different sets of financial values, and different attitudes toward money, can very readily disagree on how money is to be used. What one regards as a luxury, the other may consider a necessity.

In order to avoid difficulties in the administration of the family funds, some very basic concepts should be agreed upon at the very beginning of the marriage. First, husband and wife should constantly remind themselves that all their material possessions, whether in abundance or otherwise, really belong to God. We are merely stewards. This starting point is most important.

Second, a plan or budget for the spending and saving of the family income should be mutually decided upon. Each plan or budget must be tailored to the needs of the respective couple.

Third, the responsibility of handling the finances should be equally shared. While one does the actual handling of the funds, this does not mean that the other has no part in it, is never appraised of what is going on, or is made to feel financially dependent on the other for the most trivial things involving finances.

Achan's wedge of gold has broken many marriages asunder. The Savior, during His public ministry, never permitted riches, pleasure, or fame to interfere with the expression of His love for us. May you never permit your love for each other to be threatened or stifled by money, but rather use it as a means of expressing your love for each other.

Prayer

Lord, the eyes of all wait upon You. You open Your hands and satisfy the desire of every living thing. Because of this assurance that You have given us in Your holy Word we need not live in fear of poverty even though we do not possess great wealth. Teach us to realize that true pleasure and true security do not lie in dollars and cents, stocks and bonds, but rather in the bond that we have to You, our Provider, Protector, Redeemer. Amen.

Love Bears All Things

YOU CAN MAKE BEAUTIFUL MUSIC TOGETHER

A brief excerpt from the diary of a Christian wife and mother appeared as follows: "Nov. 29. Mary and Joe (little daughter and son), struggling with a piano duet, remind me of the early years of a marriage. Takes a lot of practice, patience, and willingness to overlook the partner's mistakes before you can make beautiful music together. Harmony doesn't come without effort."

If someone would ask you to supply in a few words the most essential ingredients that are required to establish a Christian marriage and a God-pleasing family life, you would most likely, sooner or later, come up with these Christian virtues—patience, kindness, unselfishness. Notice how each of these virtues partakes of the others. Is it possible for a person to be truly patient and yet unkind and selfish? Or is it possible for one to be filled with human kindness and at the same time be impatient and selfish?

Notice further that each of the three virtues, if truly possessed and practiced, requires a forgetting or divesting of one's self. Egocentricity—complete occupation with one's self and problems—cannot live under the same roof with patience, kindness, and unselfishness. To use the language of the marriage counselor, they are "incompatible." Egocentricity can, and often does, bring about incompatibility in marriage.

The duet that produces the perfect marriage requires perfect tempo, perfect rhythm, perfect touch, perfect expression. Your spouse does not possess all these qualities—nor do you. However, if you will see each other with the eye of patience, hear each other with the ear of kindness, and know each other with the touch of unselfishness, you will be satisfied and happy in your marriage.

The apostle Paul expresses it most beautifully: "Love is patient, love is kind. It does not envy, it does not boast, it is not proud. It is not rude, it is not self-seeking, it is not easily angered, it keeps no record of wrongs. Love does not delight in evil but rejoices with the truth. It always protects, always trusts, always hopes, always perseveres" (1 Corinthians 13:4–7).

Yes, the apostle Paul said it beautifully, and the Savior lived it perfectly—in our stead.

Prayer

Dear Savior, we pray that You will give us in our marriage relationship an abundant measure of Your perfect love. Only then will we have the patience, kindness, and unselfishness so necessary for a happy and successful marriage. When our love fails and we become intolerant of the weaknesses of the other, turn us to Yourself and each other for forgiveness and strength. Amen.

To Pray for and Encourage
Each Other—I

GOD HAS A CLAIM ON YOUR TIME, TALENT, AND TREASURE

What are the things that pertain to God? In the theological sense, all things pertain to God. Some Christian writers have put it in this way: God has full claim on our time, talents, and treasure. The way in which we respond to this claim and place our time, talents, and treasure at His disposal is called "stewardship." Every Christian is a steward (one who acts as an administrator of property for another) whether he wants to be or not. The question is, are you a good steward or a bad steward, do you practice good stewardship or bad stewardship? Furthermore, good stewardship is the responsibility of every Christian, married or single, young or old.

For reasons that are more imagined than real, good stewardship often breaks down in the initial stages of marriage. New relationships, new duties, new responsibilities tend to make the newly married couple forget that they as individuals and as a couple are a force to be used by God and not simply humans engaged in self-preservation and self-indulgence.

If God has given either of you talents as teachers, leaders, musicians, organizers, etc., then even the busy schedule of newly married life does not excuse you from placing these talents at His disposal.

The all-knowing Lord is aware that the new husband is much occupied in carving out a career in a hard, cold, competitive world. For the spiritual refreshment that he so much needs, there is only one place to find abundant supply, namely, in the service of his God and his fellow-man. He may have to make a choice between the church choir and the country club, between the service club and the Sunday school, between the poker party and parish program.

The all-knowing Lord is aware that the new wife, like Martha, is troubled about many things (see Luke 10:40) in the establishment of her new home. She may be struggling to manage both a career and a household. She too is in need of spiritual refreshment that can only be found in service to God and others.

Time and again in the New Testament the Savior warned those who desired real discipleship not to become too encumbered with the affairs of this world. We pray the same thing for each married couple when we ask that they "pray for and encourage each other in the things which pertain to God."

Prayer

O God of mercy, God of light,
In love and mercy infinite,
Teach us, as ever in Your sight,
To live our lives in You.
And may Your Holy Spirit move
All those who live to live in love
Till You receive in heav'n above
Those who have lived in You. Amen.

Lutheran Worship, 397

To Pray for and Encourage
Each Other—II

How Much Should We Give to the Church?

Our time, talents, and treasure are really possessions of God placed in our care to be used in the service of God and others.

Let us direct our attention specifically to the third "T"—treasure. Let us become even more specific in our thinking and consider how the material possessions that God has given us are to be used in His service—the stewardship of money.

You were married in God's house. He was a guest at your wedding. Then and now you feel that you want Him always as a guest in your home. In addition to the blessing that He has given you in each other, there was, as is custom, a generous outpouring of gifts at your wedding. Also, one or both of you are gainfully employed.

Now, as children of a completely unselfish God that bought you back at a tremendous price, you must together decide what portion of your material blessings you will return to Him. The pattern you set now, in the early days of your marriage, will have an immeasurable effect on the spiritual tone and atmosphere of your home.

Many Christians believe that the wise and scriptural way to arrive at the amount that is to be returned to God through the church and other deserving agencies is to give on a percentage basis. This is your way of saying to God, "When the windows of heaven open and rain down upon us abundant blessings, we want to return them to You in abundance. In the event lean years come upon us, we know that You will be pleased with a less abundant offering."

In a general way our income tax system is predicated on a percentage basis—the more you make, the more you pay. Most people feel that as long as we have to have an income tax, this system is as equitable as any. One great difference between the percentage approach in income tax and the percentage approach in Christian stewardship of money is that the first is compulsory and the latter is completely voluntary.

The good stewardship of money for your church and your Lord requires a certain amount of self-imposed discipline and sacrifice.

There will never be a more opportune time in your lives for you as husband and wife to accept the challenge of the Lord when He says, " 'Bring the whole tithe into the storehouse, that there may be food in My house. Test me in this,' says the LORD Almighty, 'and see if I will not throw open the floodgates of heaven and pour out so much blessing that you will not have room enough for it' " (Malachi 3:10).

Prayer

We give You but Your own
In any gifts we bring;
All that we have is Yours alone,
A trust from You, our King.

May we Your bounties thus
As stewards true receive
And gladly, Lord, as You bless us,
To You our first fruits give. Amen.

Lutheran Worship, 405

❧

That They May Make Their Home and Their Hearts Your Dwelling Place

RELIGION IN THE HOME

William Lyon Phelps, a great teacher, once said, "Since the greatest of all arts is the art of living together, and since the highest and most permanent values depend upon it, and since the way to practice this art successfully lies through character, the all-important question is how to obtain character. The surest way is through religion in the home."

"Religion in the home" can mean many things. The Holy Bible is as much a fixture in many American homes as the mail-order catalog. Often, in fact, the two are kept in the same bookcase and enjoy a life of undisturbed quiet under the same cover of dust. This could be regarded as having religious literature in the home, but it is not "religion in the home" in the true sense of the phrase.

In other homes, as a matter of perfunctory routine, a prayer is spoken at the beginning and end of each meal. Sometimes this becomes so perfunctory that we find people using the prayer intended for the conclusion of the meal at the beginning and vice versa. After the first few phrases have been intoned, there is an embarrassed silence and then, after sheepish grins, the proper prayer is spoken. It is in such moments that, in a most forceful way, we are brought to the startling realization that even religion can become a matter of habit.

"Religion in the home," if it has its proper place, never becomes a matter of habit. While its outward expression very often settles into a pattern of regularity (e.g., prayers on rising and retiring, before and after meals), the pattern itself should never be permitted to take the place of genuine religious experience and spiritual expression.

The religion in your home is going to be only as deep and true as the religion in your heart. Here is where husband and wife can truly support and strengthen each other. In an uninhibited way they can, and should, speak to each other about spiritual matters. They should share their thoughts about Christ, about sin and for-giveness.

Prayer

Oh, blest the house, whate'er befall,
Where Jesus Christ is all in all!
For, if He were not dwelling there,
How dark and poor and void it were!

Oh, blest that house where faith is found
And all in charity abound
To trust their God and serve Him still
And do in all His holy will! Amen.

Lutheran Worship, 467

God Blesses Those Who
Trust in Him

IN TIME OF TRIAL AND DISTRESS

Centuries ago a king, plagued by many worries, harassed on every side, called his wise men together. He asked them to invent a motto, a few magic words that would help him in time of trial or distress. It must be brief enough to be engraved on a ring, he said, so that he could have it always before his eyes. It must be appropriate to every situation.

The wise men thought and thought and finally came to the king with their magic words. They were words for every change or chance of fortune, words to fit every situation, words to ease the heart and mind in every circumstance. The motto they furnished the king was: *This, Too, Shall Pass Away.*

Think about these words for a moment and you will have to admit that they are wise and true and endlessly enduring. Paul H. Hayne, inspired by the phrase, wrote a poem bearing the same title. The poem is said to have furnished power and inspiration to countless thousands.

However, for the Christian the motto is not the complete story. There is in it, if you listen carefully, a steady undertone of futility. Is life nothing more than a series of things or incidents "passing away"? To the Christian it is infinitely more.

This motto may have been satisfactory to a pagan king, but it was only because he knew of nothing better. Christians know of something better. Something furnished, not to a king, but by a king—the King of Glory.

One day the Lord's disciples were sharing with Him a few precious moments of private, intimate discussion. They wanted to know when He would return and what the signs of His return would be. In the course of the conversation He told them: "Heaven and earth will pass away, but My words will never pass away" (Matthew 24:35).

This is by far the better motto for your marriage, because it incorporates not only the wisdom of the wise men but the promises of Almighty God.

Prayer

O Lord God, we know that the sea of matrimony is not always calm and tranquil. Hard times can, and probably will, come upon us in one form or another in the course of our marriage. May we in those days of trial and distress turn to You and Your Word, the anchor that can give stability, the compass that can give direction. Even as You have been our refuge and strength in the past, so continue Your presence in the years ahead. Amen.

Building on a Rock or on Sand?
Matthew 7:24–27

LAYING THE FOUNDATION
FOR YOUR MARRIAGE

In the seventh chapter of the Gospel According to St. Matthew Jesus tells the story of two men, one wise and one foolish. The wise man, He says, is the one who built his house on a rock, and the foolish one is the man who built his house on sand.

As you are now engaged in the lifelong project of establishing a family and building a house and a home, you can be either wise or foolish, depending on the foundation you select for the undergirding of your home.

If you build your house on sand, the preparation for the building is not nearly as arduous and the erection time is not nearly as long. By that we mean that if both of you direct all of your time and energies toward the acquiring of material things—a beautiful house, a shiny new car, and the latest styles in clothes—the appearance that you will give to the world will be one of success and achievement. But what will happen to your house if the rains of discontent, the floods of sickness, and the winds of adversity blow against it? The costly furniture, the shiny new car, and the stylish clothes will be too weak a foundation to sustain you.

Unless you build your marriage on a rock—and this can be done only by directing your time and energies to those values that are lasting and real—it is possible that your marriage may not weather the storms of life.

What are some of the stones that go into the foundation of a marriage that is solid as rock? The first stone that must be laid is that of spirituality. Unless each of you has a clear understanding of your relationship with Jesus Christ, you will find your relationship with each other difficult. The first commandment of the Decalog, "Thou shalt have no other gods before Me," is also the first commandment for a successful marriage. The material things in marriage are not evil or sand in themselves, but they can become so when not put in their proper place. What is their proper place? Jesus made it very clear when He said, "But seek first His kingdom and His righteousness, and all these things will be given to you as well" (Matthew 6:33).

A second stone that must be laid is that of unselfish love—the kind of love that is forever seeking what it might give rather than what it might receive.

In the New Testament the apostle Paul uses three different Greek words meaning love. They differ not in degree, but in kind. The first is erotic or romantic love (self-satisfying). There is some of this in your marriage, and you need not be ashamed of it. But it is only sand and not rock. The second is the type of love that two people, very intimate and close, have for each other's person and welfare (love that is returned). There should be much of this in your marriage. But it is not the rock substance needed for the foundation. The third is the deep, genuine, spiritual affection that cannot help but give and serve and even suffer in exercising itself. It does all this without looking for anything good or lovable in the object of its love.

The perfect example of this—one to which you can never attain, but for which, as husband and wife, you should always strive—is the love that drove the Savior relentlessly to the cross.

Build your marriage on these foundation stones, and you will never have to fear the floods or rain or winds of misfortune.

Prayer

Dear Lord, help us realize the truth of the hymn:

> How firm a foundation, O saints of the Lord,
> Is laid for your faith in His excellent Word!
> What more can He say than to you He has said
> Who unto the Savior for refuge have fled?
> Amen.

Lutheran Worship, 411

**Heirs with You of the Gracious
Gift of Life**
1 Peter 3:7

THIS IS JUST THE BEGINNING

Sir Hugh Walpole said it. "The most wonderful of all things in life, I believe, is the discovery of another human being with whom one's relationship has a glowing depth, beauty, and joy as the years increase. The inner progressiveness of love between two human beings is a most marvelous thing; it cannot be found by looking for it or by passionately wishing for it. It is a sort of divine accident."

We do not in any way wish to distort the beautiful thought so ably expressed by this great man of letters, but look carefully at the last sentence. Is there such a thing as a divine accident? Is it just an accident that God has brought you together as man and wife? Is it just an accident that the family you will raise and the home you will establish as Christian husband and wife will serve as a dwelling place for the Triune God with all His blessings? Is it just an accident that the joy you have known in each other, and will continue to know, is far more than you ever deserved?

If these be accidents, divine or otherwise, then they have been carefully arranged by One who has even greater plans in store for you. You are to be "heirs … of the gracious gift of life." At this point now, even in the midst of all the joy and happiness that your marriage has brought, you must try to sit back and see the whole arrangement for what it really is. Your marriage in the eyes of God is a brief period of time, a mere "moment between sun and frost," in the long pilgrimage that you are making between the poles of eternity. He claimed you as His own from the foundations of the world, and it is just a matter of time until you will be with Him in the Abiding City.

But a pilgrimage by its very nature is a difficult journey. To lighten the burden, to strengthen the body, to refresh the spirit, He has given you to each other as partners on the way.

There will be times when one will be weak and the other strong, but there will never be a time when you will not need each other.

The same Lord loves each of you with the same limitless love and stands ready to help you fill your role as husband and wife. He is so sure that your marriage will be filled with blessings that He has made you "heirs … of the gracious gift of life." Trust in Him.

Prayer

Dear Savior, You are the same yesterday, today, and forever, and with You a thousand years are but a moment in time. Raise our sights so that we may see beyond the immediate to the eternal and lasting. Cause us always to remember that our marriage was designed by You, is to be lived in Your presence, and reaches its culmination only at the marriage feast of the Lamb. To this high and noble destiny, help us, O Lord, to direct each other. Amen.